his book is to be returned on or before
last ~~~~~~ below or you will be

Life

Alan

A Good Life

Text © Alan 1977. Reprinted 1978, 1980, 1986, 1990, 1996
ISBN 0 906253 00 4
Published by Gatehouse Books, Hulme Adult Education Centre,
Hulme Walk, Manchester M15 5FQ
Photographs: cover, thanks to Manchester Central Library Local Studies
Unit, and to Paula Moorehouse. P. 7, The Yorkshire Miner.
Illustrations by John
Typesetting and design: Peter Findlay and Tom Woodin.
Beginner reader cover design: David Andrassy
Printing: RAP, 201 Spotland Road, Rochdale (01706 44981)
Gatehouse is a charity registered in England no. 1011042
Gatehouse gratefully acknowledges the financial support of Manchester
City Council and North West Arts Board.
Gatehouse is a member of the Federation of Worker Writers and
Community Publishers (FWWCP).

SCHOOL

It was just simply

the teachers had no time for you.

You sat in a row

and you got to read a book.

You get hold of a book.

Everyone gets hold of a book.

They start from the front.

One reads one line.

The second pupil reads the second line,

and so on.

And when it gets to you,

if you can't read it

he just says,

"Right, forget about you.
Go over to the next one."
And, you know he's going along,
and say there's somebody
else like you,
he just says,
"Forget about you,"
and goes over to the next one.
And that's how it went on.

WORK

I went working for a plumbers
in property.
I started working for a firm
for £1-4-6d a week.
I give my mother a pound.
I had 4s-6d.
I stopped there till I was 18.
I had the choice,
either go in the national service,
two years in the army,
or go and be a Bevin boy*,
that's working in the coal mines.

*Named after Ernest Bevin. He had set up this scheme
up during the 1939-45 war.

So I went in the coal mines

when I was 18.

From 18 till I was 27

I had to stop in the mines,

9 years.

I stopped in the mines

till I was 27.

(You're getting to know my age now!)

After that

I came out

and I was just messing about.

I went on the docks.

On the docks I earned very good money.

I invested the money.

DOWN THE MINES

When you're single
you get about £5 a day.
Five days a week - £25.
You give your parents so much for living on.
You buy yourself a car.
You go away for the weekend.
You come back on Monday morning
ready for work again.
I was on the coal face,
getting coal off the coal face.

These days they have modern gadgets.

Those days you had to hand-ball it.

That means shovel it.

You got frightened,

but what the hell could you do about it?

So I come out of the mines,

have my family and my kids,

and I have a good life.

HOW TO GET RICH

I work on the docks, right.

I work long hours.

I have money off the job,-

say £50, £60, £70 a week.

I don't know what to do with it.

I can't put it in the bank,

because I can't read,

or write a form out

to put the money in.

So I keep it in my pocket.

You get about £200 to £300 in your pocket,

and what can you do with it?

Before.

You can either burn it,
or do something with it.
And the only thing I did was,
I had a look round,
I saw a house,
I bought that house.

I got some more good jobs off the docks.

I got some more good money.

I bought some furniture.

I bought material

for doing the old house up.

When the house was done up,

I let it off.

Got some more money off the docks,

with working hard.

Bought another house,

and that's how it kept on going.

Gatehouse Books

Gatehouse is a unique publisher
Our writers are adults who are developing their basic
reading and writing skills. Their ideas and experiences
make fascinating material for any reader, but are
particularly relevant for adults working on their reading
and writing skills. The writing strikes a chord - a shared
experience of struggling against many odds.

The format of our books is clear and uncluttered. The
language is familiar and the text is often line-broken, so
that each line ends at a natural pause.

Gatehouse books are both popular and respected within
Adult Basic Education throughout the English speaking
world. They are also a valuable resource within
secondary schools, Social Services and within the Prison
Education Service and Probation Services.

Booklist available

Gatehouse Books
Hulme Adult Education Centre
Hulme Walk
Manchester
M15 5FQ
Tel: 0161 226 7152
Fax: 0161 226 8854

The Gatehouse Publishing Charity Ltd is a registered charity, no. 1011042
Gatehouse Books Ltd is a company limited by guarantee, reg no. 2619614